D1241322

Given

Also by Wendell Berry

FICTION
Fidelity
Jayber Crow
Hannah Coulter
The Memory of Old Jack
Nathan Coulter
A Place on Earth
Remembering
That Distant Land
Watch With Me
The Wild Birds
A World Lost

POETRY
The Broken Ground
Clearing
Collected Poems: 1957–1982
The Country of Marriage
Entries
Farming: A Hand Book
Findings
Openings
A Part
Sabbaths
Sayings and Doings
The Selected Poems of Wendell Berry (1998)
A Timbered Choir
The Wheel

ESSAYS
Another Turn of the Crank
The Art of the Commonplace
Citizenship Papers
A Continuous Harmony
The Gift of Good Land
Harlan Hubbard: Life and Work
The Hidden Wound
Home Economics
Life Is a Miracle
Long-Legged House
Recollected Essays: 1965–1980
Sex, Economy, Freedom and Community
Standing by Words
The Unforeseen Wilderness
The Unsettling of America
What Are People For?

Given

New Poems

Wendell Berry

Shoemaker  Hoard, Washington, D.C.

Copyright © 2005 by Wendell Berry

All rights reserved. No part of this book may be used or
reproduced in any manner whatsoever without written permission
from the Publisher, except in the case of brief quotations embodied
in critical articles and reviews.

Library of Congress Cataloging-in-Publication Data
Berry, Wendell, 1934-
Given : new poems / Wendell Berry.
p. cm.
Includes bibliographical references and index.
ISBN 1-59376-061-2 (alk. paper)
I. Title.
PS3552.E75G58 2005
811'.54 — dc22   2005003762

Text design by David Bullen
Printed in the United States of America

Shoemaker ⬛ Hoard
A Division of Avalon Publishing Group, Inc.
Distributed by Publishers Group West

10 9 8 7 6 5 4 3 2 1

In memory: Ross Feld

CONTENTS

Part I:

In a Country Once Forested

DUST

The dust motes float
and swerve in the sunbeam,
as lively as worlds,
and I remember my brother
when we were boys:
"We may be living on an atom
in somebody's wallpaper."

IN A COUNTRY ONCE FORESTED

The young woodland remembers
the old, a dreamer dreaming

of an old holy book,
an old set of instructions,

and the soil under the grass
is dreaming of a young forest,

and under the pavement the soil
is dreaming of grass.

SPRING HAIKU

1.
One young wild plum tree,
White in the bare woods, a bride
Among wedding guests.

2.
Mayapples: a crowd
Hidden under umbrellas
In the falling rain.

3.
The lilac blossoms
all suddenly are fallen—
how bright a shadow!

TO TANYA ON MY SIXTIETH BIRTHDAY

What wonder have you done to me?
In binding love you set me free.
These sixty years the wonder prove:
I bring you aged a young man's love.

THEY

I see you down there, white-haired
among the green leaves,
picking the ripe raspberries,
and I think, "Forty-two years!"
We are the you and I who were
they whom we remember.

CATHEDRAL

Stone
of the earth
made
of its own weight
light

DANTE

If you imagine
others are there,
you are there yourself.

ALL

All bend
in one wind.

THE FACT

After all these
analyses,
the fact
remains intact.

THE MILLENNIUM

What year
does the phoebe
think it is?

JUNE WIND

Light and wind are running
over the headed grass
as though the hill had
melted and now flowed.

A SMALL THEOLOGY

"With God all things are possible"—
that's the beginning and the end
of theology. If all things are possible,
nothing is impossible.
Why do the godly then
keep slinging out their nooses?

WHY

Why all the embarrassment
about being happy?
Sometimes I'm as happy
as a sleeping dog,
and for the same reasons,
and for others.

THE REJECTED HUSBAND

After the storm and the new
stillness of the snow, he returns
to the graveyard, as though
he might lift the white coverlet,
slip in beside her as he used to do,
and again feel, beneath his hand,
her flesh quicken and turn warm.
But he is not her husband now.
To participate in resurrection, one
first must be dead. And he goes
back into the whitened world, alive.

THE INLET

In a dream I go
out into the sunlit street
and I see a boy walking
clear-eyed in the light.
I recognize him, he is
Bill Lippert, wearing the gray
uniform of the school
we attended many years ago.
And then I see that my brother
is with me in the dream,
dressed too in the old uniform.
Our friend looks as he did
when we first knew him,
and until I wake I believe
I will die of grief, for I know
that this boy grew into a man
who was a faithful friend
who died.
          Where I stood,
seeing and knowing, was time,
where we die of grief. And surely
the bright street of my dream,
in which we saw again
our old friend as a boy
clear-eyed in innocence of his death,
was some quickly-crossed
small inlet of eternity.

LISTEN!

How fine to have a radio
and beautiful music playing
while I sit at rest in the evening.
How fine to hear through the music
the cries of wild geese on the river.

In Art Rowanberry's barn, when Art's death
had become quietly a fact among
the other facts, Andy Catlett found
a jacket made of the top half
of a pair of coveralls after
the legs wore out, for Art
never wasted anything.
Andy found a careful box made
of woodscraps with a strap
for a handle; it contained
a handful of small nails
wrapped in a piece of newspaper,
several large nails, several
rusty bolts with nuts and washers,
some old harness buckles
and rings, rusty but usable,
several small metal boxes, empty,
and three hickory nuts
hollowed out by mice.
And all of these things Andy
put back where they had been,
for time and the world and other people
to dispense with as they might,
but not by him to be disprized.
This long putting away
of things maybe useful was not all
of Art's care-taking; he cared
for creatures also, every day
leaving his tracks in dust, mud,

or snow as he went about
looking after his stock, or gave
strength to lighten a neighbor's work.
Andy found a bridle made
of several lengths of baling twine
knotted to a rusty bit,
an old set of chain harness,
four horseshoes of different sizes,
and three hammerstones picked up
from the opened furrow on days
now as perfectly forgotten
as the days when they were lost.
He found a good farrier's knife,
an awl, a key to a lock
that would no longer open.

A STONE JUG

A bulldozer digging a pond
on my mother's family's land
unearths two stoneware jugs
buried four feet in the ground,
one broken and one intact.
Who put them there? When? Why?
We suppose, but can't explain.
Those who have come and gone
are gone. How lost to us
they are whose lives passed here
in the sun's beauty and sorrow!
And who in a hundred years
will know us as we are
in our present living and dying
here under the very sun, lost
to the future as to the past?

BURLEY COULTER'S SONG
FOR KATE HELEN BRANCH

The rugs were rolled back to the wall,
The band in place, the lamps all lit.
We talked and laughed a little bit
And then obeyed the caller's call—
Light-footed, happy, half entranced—
To balance, swing, and promenade.
Do you remember how we danced
And how the fiddler played?

About midnight we left the crowd
And wandered out to take a stroll.
We heard the treefrogs and the owl;
Nearby the creek was running loud.
The good dark held us as we chanced
The joy we two together made,
Remembering how we'd whirled and pranced
And how the fiddler played.

That night is many years ago
And gone, and still I see you clear,
Clear as the lamplight in your hair.
The old time comes around me now,
And I remember how you glanced
At me, and how we stepped and swayed.
I can't forget the way we danced,
The way the fiddler played.

HOW TO BE A POET
(to remind myself)

Make a place to sit down.
Sit down. Be quiet.
You must depend upon
affection, reading, knowledge,
skill—more of each
than you have—inspiration,
work, growing older, patience,
for patience joins time
to eternity. Any readers
who like your work,
doubt their judgment.

Breathe with unconditional breath
the unconditioned air.
Shun electric wire.
Communicate slowly. Live
a three-dimensioned life;
stay away from screens.
Stay away from anything
that obscures the place it is in.
There are no unsacred places;
there are only sacred places
and desecrated places.

Accept what comes from silence.
Make the best you can of it.
Of the little words that come
out of the silence, like prayers
prayed back to the one who prays,
make a poem that does not disturb
the silence from which it came.

WORDS

1.

What is one to make of a life given
to putting things into words,
saying them, writing them down?
Is there a world beyond words?
There is. But don't start, don't
go on about the tree unqualified,
standing in light that shines
to time's end beyond its summoning
name. Don't praise the speechless
starlight, the unspeakable dawn.
Just stop.

2.

      Well, we *can* stop
for a while, if we try hard enough,
if we are lucky. We can sit still,
keep silent, let the phoebe, the sycamore,
the river, the stone call themselves
by whatever they call themselves, their own
sounds, their own silence, and thus
may know for a moment the nearness
of the world, its vastness,
its vast variousness, far and near,
which only silence knows. And then
we must call all things by name
out of the silence again to be with us,
or die of namelessness.

TO A WRITER OF REPUTATION

. . . the man must remain obscure.
Cézanne

Having begun in public anonymity,
you did not count on this
literary sublimation by which
some body becomes a "name"—
as if you have died and have become
a part of mere geography. Greet,
therefore, the roadsigns on the road.

Or perhaps you have become deaf and blind,
or merely inanimate, and may
be studied without embarrassment
by the disinterested, the dispassionate,
and the merely curious,
not fearing to be overheard.
Hello to the grass, then, and to the trees.

Or perhaps you are secretly
still alert and moving, no longer the one
they have named, but another,
named by yourself,
carrying away this morning's showers
for your private delectation.
Hello, river.

Part II:

Further Words

SEVENTY YEARS

Well, anyhow, I am
not going to die young.

A POSITION

I'm philosophically opposed to iced drinks:
Last should equal first, for a man who thinks.

A PASSING THOUGHT

I think therefore
I think I am.

THE LEADER

Head like a big
watermelon,
frequently thumped
and still not ripe.

THE ONGOING HOLY WAR AGAINST EVIL

Stop the killing, or
I'll kill you, you
God-damned murderer!

For God's sake, be done
with this jabber of "a better world."
What blasphemy! No "futuristic"
twit or child thereof ever
in embodied light will see
a better world than this, though they
foretell inevitably a worse.
Do something! Go cut the weeds
beside the oblivious road. Pick up
the cans and bottles, old tires,
and dead predictions. No future
can be stuffed into this presence
except by being dead. The day is
clear and bright, and overhead
the sun not yet half finished
with his daily praise.

SOME FURTHER WORDS

Let me be plain with you, dear reader.
I am an old-fashioned man. I like
the world of nature despite its mortal
dangers. I like the domestic world
of humans, so long as it pays its debts
to the natural world, and keeps its bounds.
I like the promise of Heaven. My purpose
is a language that can pay just thanks
and honor for those gifts, a tongue
set free from fashionable lies.

Neither this world nor any of its places
is an "environment." And a house
for sale is not a "home." Economics
is not "science," nor "information" knowledge.
A knave with a degree is a knave. A fool
in a public office is not a "leader."
A rich thief is a thief. And the ghost
of Arthur Moore, who taught me Chaucer,
returns in the night to say again:
"Let me tell you something, boy.
An intellectual whore is a whore."

The world is babbled to pieces after
the divorce of things from their names.
Ceaseless preparation for war
is not peace. Health is not procured
by sale of medication, or purity
by the addition of poison. Science

at the bidding of the corporations
is knowledge reduced to merchandise;
it is a whoredom of the mind,
and so is the art that calls this "progress."
So is the cowardice that calls it "inevitable."

I think the issues of "identity" mostly
are poppycock. We are what we have done,
which includes our promises, includes
our hopes, but promises first. I know
a "fetus" is a human child.
I loved my children from the time
they were conceived, having loved
their mother, who loved them
from the time they were conceived
and before. Who are we to say
the world did not begin in love?

I would like to die in love as I was born,
and as myself, of life impoverished, go
into the love all flesh begins
and ends in. I don't like machines,
which are neither mortal nor immortal,
though I am constrained to use them.
(Thus the age perfects its clench.)
Some day they will be gone, and that
will be a glad and a holy day.
I mean the dire machines that run
by burning the world's body and
its breath. When I see an airplane
fuming through the once-pure sky

or a vehicle of the outer space
with its little inner space
imitating a star at night, I say,
"Get *out* of there!" as I would speak
to a fox or a thief in the henhouse.

When I hear the stock market has fallen,
I say, "Long live gravity! Long live
stupidity, error, and greed in the palaces
of fantasy capitalism!" I think
an economy should be based on thrift,
on taking care of things, not on theft,
usury, seduction, waste, and ruin.

My purpose is a language that can make us whole,
though mortal, ignorant, and small.
The world is whole beyond human knowing.
The body's life is its own, untouched
by the little clockwork of explanation.
I approve of death, when it comes in time
to the old. I don't want to live
on mortal terms forever, or survive
an hour as a cooling stew of pieces
of other people. I don't believe that life
or knowledge can be given by machines.
The machine economy has set afire
the household of the human soul,
and all the creatures are burning within it.

"Intellectual property" names
the deed by which the mind is bought

and sold, the world enslaved. We
who do not own ourselves, being free,
own by theft what belongs to God,
to the living world, and equally
to us all. Or how can we own a part
of what we only can possess entirely?
"The laborer is worthy of his hire,"
but he cannot own what he knows,
which must be freely told, or labor
dies with the laborer. The farmer
is worthy of the harvest made
in time, but he must leave the light
by which he planted, grew, and reaped,
the seed immortal in mortality,
freely to the time to come. The land
too he keeps by giving it up,
as the thinker receives and gives a thought,
as the singer sings in the common air.

I don't believe that "scientific genius"
in its naïve assertions of power
is equal either to nature or
to human culture. Its thoughtless invasions
of the nuclei of atoms and cells
and this world's every habitation
have not brought us to the light
but sent us wandering farther through
the dark. Nor do I believe
"artistic genius" is the possession
of any artist. No one has made
the art by which one makes the works

of art. Each one who speaks speaks
as a convocation. We live as councils
of ghosts. It is not "human genius"
that makes us human, but an old love,
an old intelligence of the heart
we gather to us from the world,
from the creatures, from the angels
of inspiration, from the dead—
an intelligence merely nonexistent
to those who do not have it, but
to those who have it more dear than life.

And just as tenderly to be known
are the affections that make a woman and a man,
their household, and their homeland one.
These too, though known, cannot be told
to those who do not know them, and fewer
of us learn them, year by year,
loves that are leaving the world
like the colors of extinct birds,
like the songs of a dead language.

Think of the genius of the animals,
every one truly what it is:
gnat, fox, minnow, swallow, each made
of light and luminous within itself.
They know (better than we do) how
to live in the places where they live.
And so I would like to be a true
human being, dear reader—a choice
not altogether possible now.

But this is what I'm for, the side
I'm on. And this is what you should
expect of me, as I expect it of myself,
though for realization we may wait
a thousand or a million years.

LYSIMACHIA NUMMULARIA

It is called moneywort
for its "coinlike" leaves
and perhaps its golden flowers.
I love it because it is
a naturalized exotic
that does no harm,
and for its lowly thriving,
and for its actual
unlikeness to money.

ORIGINAL SIN

Well, anyhow, it preserves us from the pride
of thinking we invented sin ourselves
by our originality, that famous modern power.
In fact, we have it from the beginning
of the world by the errors of being born,
being young, being old, causing pain
to ourselves, to others, to the world, to God
by ignorance, by knowledge, by intention,
by accident. Something is bad the matter
here, informing us of itself, handing down
its old instruction. We know it
when we see it, don't we? Innocence
would never recognize it. We need it
too, for without it we would not know
forgiveness, goodness, gratitude,
that fund of grace by which alone we live.

Part III:

Sonata at Payne Hollow

The Kentucky shore of the Ohio at evening. Some time in the future, perhaps a saner time than now. It is the season when the toads mate and sing from the stones along the water's edge at night. Here the river has curved in close to the foot of a steep hillside. The slope is wooded with tall trees. A fringe of willows along the shoreline opens to give a view up among the larger trunks. During the play, the light slowly changes from twilight to dusk.

Two boatmen, a man past middle age and a boy of about fifteen, come ashore. They may be small-time traders who row or drift from one river town to another. Their johnboat, the bow of which is visible to our right, is of the traditional make, built of wood. A rope is attached to a ring in the bow.

The boy carries the end of the rope up the shore and makes it fast to a willow. He then stands and looks around.

THE BOY:

We never stopped here before.

THE MAN:

Night never caught us here before.
But look. There is the notch in the hill,
and there is the creek coming down,
and here are the rocks it has brought
and shaped in a little bar fanned out
on the river's edge. You've heard of this place.
Up yonder on the slope is where they lived
and made their music, in a house
built of rocks and poles and rough planks
and pieces of drift from the river.

THE BOY:

Who were they? Tell me again.

THE MAN:

Their names were Harlan and Anna.
A long time ago they came here,
past the middle of their lives, to live
until they were old. They were refugees
from that violent world of our ancestors
that nearly destroyed itself. They wanted
a quiet place that was dark at night, unwanted
by other people, where they could grow their food
or catch or find it, and be warmed by firewood
burning on a hearth they made of rocks
carried up from the river or the creek.
Harlan, they say, made pictures of the river
and the trees and little farms that stood
along the valley sides. And he and Anna
made fine music in the evenings
with his fiddle and her piano. Up there
is where their house was, and there
the little shop where he made the pictures,
and there the shed where they kept their goats.

THE BOY:

And that was long ago?

THE MAN:

                  Long ago.
The boards of their buildings now
are gone to dust, and trees are standing
where they played and ate and slept.

THE BOY:

What became of them?

THE MAN:

                  They got old,

and died. And yonder, below the chimney stones,
is where they were laid to rest—or not,
maybe, to rest. For there's them that tells
of being here at night, and hearing that old music
strike up sudden in the woods, and seeing
those two ancient lovers walking about, talking.

THE BOY:

Oh, Lord! Talking! What do they say?

THE MAN:

They talk of what they could not talk about
enough while they were here, like all ghosts do.

THE BOY:

If it was up to me to choose,
I'd just as soon be someplace else.
Your talk is talk enough for me.

THE MAN:

There ain't no harm in them.
There wasn't but little, if any, in them
when they were living on this earth,
and there's not any in them now.
Listen!

THE BOY:

       What? Is it them?

THE MAN:

It's them. You needn't be afraid.
We're not where they are.

THE BOY:

               But
they're where we are.

THE MAN:

          Be still!

Now, as from far off among the trees, we hear a piano and violin—perhaps it is Mozart's Sonata in E-flat Major. The piano is played with elegance and technical precision. The quality of the violin, by contrast, is "honest and handmade" but "strikes deep." The sound of the toads has ceased. The music, at first only faintly audible, becomes louder. Now there can be no doubt what it is. The man and boy stand still, listening, the boy looking a little anxiously at the man.

Now, slowly, candlelight defines a large window among the trees well up the slope.

And now, with the light fading off the boatman and his boy, the figure of a slender, white-haired old man is revealed, standing by the river's edge upstream. We have not seen him come; he is just there, perhaps having been there for some time. He stands, facing upstream, his left side to the river and to us, looking out across the slowly darkening water. The knuckles of his half-open left hand rest against his hip.

And now the light defines the shape of an old woman walking among the trees. She crosses above the old man and comes slowly down to the water's edge, where she too stands still, looking out, her left hand holding to a small willow. She faces downstream, her right side to us. Except for the music, the scene becomes completely still. The stillness is allowed to establish itself before Anna speaks.

In the dialogue that follows, the differences are expressed with feeling, but not with antipathy or anger. What we are witnessing is a ritual of courtship, discord reenacted as for pleasure, the outcome foreknown. Perhaps it has been repeated countless times before.

ANNA:

There you are, Harlan. I've called
and called. What are you doing?

HARLAN:

Looking.

ANNA:

At what?

HARLAN:

The river.

ANNA:

You've never seen enough, have you,
of that river you looked at all your life?

HARLAN:

It never does anything twice. It needs
forever to be in all its times and aspects
and acts. To know it in time is only
to begin to know it. To paint it, you must
show it as less than it is. That is why
as a painter I never was at rest. Now
I look and do not paint. This is the heaven
of a painter—only to look, to see
without limit. It's as if a poet finally
were free to say only the simplest things.

*For a moment they are still again, both continuing to look, in
opposite directions, at the river.*

ANNA:

That is our music, Harlan.
Do you hear it?

HARLAN:

Yes, I hear.

ANNA:

I think it will always be here.
It draws us back out of eternity
as once it drew us together
in time. Do you remember, Harlan,
how we played? And how, in playing,
we no longer needed to say
what we needed to say?

HARLAN:

I'm listening.

But I heard here too, remember,
another music, farther off,
more solitary, closer—

ANNA:

To what, Harlan?

HARLAN:

I'm not so sure I ever knew.
Closer to the edge of modern life,
I suppose—to where the life
of living things actually is lived;
closer to the beauty that saves
and consoles this earth. I wanted
to spend whole days watching
the little fish that flicker along the shore.

ANNA:

Yes. I know you did.

HARLAN:

I wanted
to watch, every morning forever,

the world shape itself again
out of the drifting fog.

ANNA:

Your music,
then, was it in those things?

HARLAN:

It was in them and beyond them,
always almost out of hearing.

ANNA:

Because of it you made
the beautiful things you made,
for yourself alone, and yet,
I think, for us both. You made
them for us both, as for yourself,
for what we were together
required those things of you alone.

HARLAN:

To hear that music, I needed
to be alone and free.

ANNA:

Free, Harlan?

HARLAN:

I longed for the perfection of the single
one. When the river rose and the current
fled by, I longed to cast myself adrift,
to take that long, free downward-flowing
as my own. I knew the longing
of an old rooted tree to lean down
upon the water.

ANNA:

I know that.

I knew that all along. And then
was when I loved you most.
What brought me to you was knowing
the long, solitary journey that was
you, yourself—the thought of you
in a little boat, adrift and free.
But, Harlan, why did you never go?
Why did you not just drift away,
solitary and free, living on the free
charity of the seasons, wintering in caves
as sometimes you said you'd like to do?

HARLAN:

Oh, Anna, because I was lonely!
The perfection of the single one
is not perfection, for it is lonely.

ANNA:

From longing for the perfection
of the single one, I called you
into longing for the perfection
of the union of two,

HARLAN:

                    which also was
imperfect, for we were not always at one,
and I never ceased, quite, to long
for solitude.

ANNA:

            And yet, of the two
imperfections, the imperfection of the union
of two is by far the greater and finer—
as we understood.

HARLAN:

                  Yes, my dear Anna,
that I too understood. It is better,
granting imperfection in both ways,
to be imperfect and together
than to be imperfect and alone.

ANNA:

And so this is the heaven of lovers
that we have come to—to live again
in our separateness, so that we may
live again together, my Harlan.

HARLAN:

And so we named a day—remember?—
and a certain train that you would be on
if you wanted to marry me,

ANNA:

                        and that you
would be on if you wanted to marry me,

BOTH:

and both of us were on that train!

ANNA:

And then, Harlan, we did drift away

HARLAN:

on a little boat we built ourselves,
that contained hardly more than our music,
our stove, our table, and our bed

ANNA:

in which we slept—and did not sleep—

HARLAN:

my birthplace into our new life!

ANNA:

For a long time we had no home
but that little boat and one another

HARLAN:

and the music that we sent forth
over the water and into the woods.

ANNA:

And then we came here to this hollow
and built a house and made a garden

HARLAN:

and gave our life a standing place
and worked and played and lived and died

ANNA:

and were alone and were not alone.

HARLAN:

Alone and not alone, we lived and died,
and after your death I lived on
alone, yet not alone, for in my thoughts
I never ceased to speak with you.
I knew then that half my music
was hidden away in another world.
The music I had heard, so distant,
had been the music you and I had played—
the music of something almost whole
that you and I had made; it made
one thing of food and hunger, work
and rest, day and night. It made
one thing of loneliness and love.
That music seemed another world
to me, and far away, because
I could play only half, not all.

ANNA:

> And half the life that you so longed
> to live—was mine?

HARLAN:

>   Was yours. Without you,
> I could not live the life we lived,
> which I then missed and longed for,
> even in my perfect solitude.

ANNA:

> You will forgive, I hope, my pleasure
> in the thought of you alone, playing
> half a duet—for also it saddens me.

HARLAN:

> You would have laughed, Anna,
> to hear how badly I played alone,
> without your strong art to carry me.
> My perfect music then was made
> by crickets and katydids and frogs.
> I heard too the creek always coming down,
> allegro furioso after storms,
> and of course the birds—the wood thrush,
> whose song in summer twilight
> renews the world, and in all seasons
> the wren. But those unceasing voices
> in the dark were the ones that sang for me,
> and I was thankful for the loneliness
> that had brought us two together
> out of all the time we were apart.

*And now, as both have known they would, they turn toward
one another, and thus are changed, revealing themselves now as*

neither young nor old, but timeless and clear, as each appears within the long affection of the other.

With this (their only movement since their conversation began), the light on them brightens and changes; it becomes, for only a moment, the brilliance of a spring morning, and on the slope, where before only the candlelit window showed among the trees, now appears the house as it was, with a garden on the terrace below. Harlan and Anna smile and lift their arms toward one another. And then they and the light abruptly disappear. The music stops. The trilling of the toads is audible again, and we see the boatman and his boy looking up the darkening hillside. The boy turns toward the man and is preparing to speak when the stage goes entirely dark. The toads sing on another moment, and then are silenced.

PRODUCTION NOTE: The left side of Harlan's face and the right side of Anna's are made up to appear old. The opposite sides of their faces should denote, not youth, but the youthful maturity of a couple in their forties—faces lovely because they are lovely to one another.

Part IV:

Sabbaths 1998–2004

Sabbaths 1998

I

Whatever happens,
those who have learned
to love one another
have made their way
to the lasting world
and will not leave,
whatever happens.

II

This is the time you'd like to stay.
Not a leaf stirs. There is no sound.
The fireflies lift light from the ground.
You've shed the vanities of when
And how and why, for now. And then
The phone rings. You are called away.

III

Early in the morning, walking
in a garden in Vancouver
three thousand miles from your grave,
the sky dripping, song
sparrows singing in the borders,
I come suddenly upon
a Japanese dogwood, a tree
you loved, bowed down with bloom.
By what blessedness do I weep?

IV

The woods and pastures are joyous
in their abundance now
in a season of warmth and much rain.
We walk amidst foliage, amidst
song. The sheep and cattle graze
like souls in bliss (except for flies)
and lie down satisfied. Who now
can believe in winter? In winter
who could have hoped for this?

V

In a single motion the river comes and goes.
At times, living beside it, we hardly notice it
as it noses calmly along within its bounds
like the family pig. But a day comes
when it swiftens, darkens, rises, flows over
its banks, spreading its mirrors out upon
the flat fields of the valley floor, and then
it is like God's love or sorrow, including
at last all that had been left out.

VI

By expenditure of hope,
Intelligence, and work,
You think you have it fixed.
It is unfixed by rule.
Within the darkness, all
Is being changed, and you
Also will be changed.

Now I recall to mind
A costly year: Jane Kenyon,
Bill Lippert, Philip Sherrard,
All in the same spring dead,
So much companionship
Gone as the river goes.

And my good workhorse Nick
Dead, who called out to me
In his conclusive pain
To ask my help. I had
No help to give. And flood
Covered the cropland twice.
By summer's end there are
No more perfect leaves.

*

But won't you be ashamed
To count the passing year
At its mere cost, your debt
Inevitably paid?

For every year is costly,
As you know well. Nothing
Is given that is not
Taken, and nothing taken
That was not first a gift.

The gift is balanced by
Its total loss, and yet,
And yet the light breaks in,
Heaven seizing its moments
That are at once its own
And yours. The day ends
And is unending where
The summer tanager,
Warbler, and vireo
Sing as they move among
Illuminated leaves.

VII
For John Haines

There is a place you can go
where you are quiet,
a place of water and the light

on the water. Trees are there,
leaves, and the light
on leaves moved by air.

Birds, singing, move
among leaves, in leaf shadow.
After many years you have come

to no thought of these,
but they are themselves
your thoughts. There seems to be

little to say, less and less.
Here they are. Here you are.
Here as though gone.

None of us stays, but in the hush
where each leaf in the speech
of leaves is a sufficient syllable

the passing light finds out
surpassing freedom of its way.

VIII

Given the solemn river,
given the trees along the banks,
given the summer warmth,
the evening light—what
could have foretold the sudden
apparition of these two
speeding by as if late
for the world's end, their engine
shaking the air, breaking
the water's mirrors?
The trees and the sky hush
with dismay, and then,
upon the return of reflection,
with sorrow. How many years
of labor to become completely
anomalous everywhere?

IX

What I fear most is despair
for the world and us: forever less
of beauty, silence, open air,
gratitude, unbidden happiness,
affection, unegotistical desire.

X

Tanya. Now that I am getting old,
I feel I must hurry against time to tell you
(as long ago I started out to do) everything,

though I know that really there can be no end
to all there is for me to say to you even of this,
our temporary life. Sometimes it seems to me

that I am divided from you by a shadow
of incomprehension, mine or yours, or mine and yours;
or that I am caught in the misery of selfhood

forever. And I think that this must be
the lot (may God help us) of all mortals who love
each other: to know by truth that they do so,

but also by error. Often now I am reminded
that the time may come (for this is our pledge)
when you will stand by me and know

that I, though "living" still, have gone beyond
all remembering, as my father went in time
before me; or that I have gone, like my mother,

into a time of pain, drugs, and still sleep.
But I know now that in that great distance
on the edge or beyond the edge of this world

I will be growing alight with being. And (listen!)
I will be longing to come back. This
came to me in a dream, near morning,

after I had labored through the night under
this weight of earthly love. On time's edge, wakened,
shaken, light and free, I will be longing

to return, to seek you through the world,
to find you (recognizing you by your beauty),
to marry you, to make a place to live,

to have children and grandchildren. The light
of that place beyond time will show me the world
as perhaps Christ saw it before His birth

in the stable at Bethlehem. I will see that it is
imperfect. It will be imperfect. (To whom would love
appear but to those in most desperate need?) Yes,

we would err again. Yes, we would suffer
again. Yes, provided you would have it
so, I would do it all again.

Sabbaths 1999

I

Can I see the buds that are swelling
in the woods on the slopes
on the far side of the valley? I can't,
of course, nor can I see
the twinleafs and anemones
that are blooming over there
bright-scattered above the dead
leaves. But the swelling buds
and little blossoms make
a new softness in the light
that is visible all the way here.
The trees, the hills that were stark
in the old cold become now
tender, and the light changes.

II

I dream of a quiet man
who explains nothing and defends
nothing, but only knows
where the rarest wildflowers
are blooming, and who goes,
and finds that he is smiling
not by his own will.

III

The spring woods hastening now
To overshadow him,
He's passing in to where
He can't see out. It charms
Mere eyesight to believe
The nearest thing not trees
Is the sky, into which
The trees reach, opening
Their luminous new leaves.
Burdened only by
A weightless shawl of shade
The lighted leaves let fall,
He seems to move within
A form unpatterned to
His eye or mind, design
Betokened to his thought
By leafshapes tossed about.
Ways untranslatable
To human tongue or hand
Seem tangled here, and yet
Are brought to light, are brought
To life, and thought finds rest
Beneath a brightened tree
In which, unseen, a warbler
Feeds and sings. His song's
Small shapely melody
Comes down irregularly,
As all light's givings come.

IV

What a consolation it is, after
the explanations and the predictions
of further explanations still
to come, to return unpersuaded
to the woods, entering again
the presence of the blessed trees.
A tree forms itself in answer
to its place and to the light.
Explain it how you will, the only
thing explainable will be
your explanation. There is
in the woods on a summer's
morning, birdsong all around
from guess where, nowhere
that rigid measure which predicts
only humankind's demise.

V

In Heaven the starry saints will wipe away
The tears forever from our eyes, but they
Must not erase the memory of our grief.
In bliss, even, there can be no relief
If we forget this place, shade-haunted, parched
Or flooded, dark or bright, where we have watched
The world always becoming what it is,
Splendor and woe surpassing happiness
Or sorrow, loss sweeping it as a floor.
This shadowed passage between door and door
Is half-lit by old words we've heard or read.
As the living recall the dead, the dead
Are joyless until they call back their lives:
Fallen like leaves, the husbands and the wives
In history's ignorant, bloody to-and-fro,
Eternally in love, and in time learning so.

VI

We travelers, walking to the sun, can't see
Ahead, but looking back the very light
That blinded us shows us the way we came,
Along which blessings now appear, risen
As if from sightlessness to sight, and we,
By blessing brightly lit, keep going toward
That blessed light that yet to us is dark.

VII

Again I resume the long
lesson: how small a thing
can be pleasing, how little
in this hard world it takes
to satisfy the mind
and bring it to its rest.

Within the ongoing havoc
the woods this morning is
almost unnaturally still.
Through stalled air, unshadowed
light, a few leaves fall
of their own weight.

                The sky
is gray. It begins in mist
almost at the ground
and rises forever. The trees
rise in silence almost
natural, but not quite,
almost eternal, but
not quite.
          What more did I
think I wanted? Here is
what has always been.
Here is what will always
be. Even in me,
the Maker of all this
returns in rest, even

to the slightest of His works,
a yellow leaf slowly
falling, and is pleased.

VIII

The difference is a polished
blade, edgewise to the eye.
On one side gleams the sun
of time, and on the other
the never-fading light,
and so the tree that stands
full-leaved in broad day
and the darkness following
stands also in the eye
of Love and is never darkened.

The blade that divides these lights
mirrors both—is one.
Time and eternity
stand in the same day
which is now in time, and forever
now. How do we know?
We know. We know we know.
They only truly live
who are the comforted.

IX

The incarnate Word is with us,
is still speaking, is present
always, yet leaves no sign
but everything that is.

Sabbaths 2000

I

In the world forever one
With the informing Love
That gives its life to time,

In the day of alchemy,
Come round at last, transmuting
Corruption to pollution,

Transmuting lies to blindness,
And light to dark, the known
Destroyed in our unknowing,

Under the sun that shines
Beyond evil and good,
The goldeneye alights

On the cold river. Grace
Unasked, merely allowed,
Gleams round him on the water.

II

When we convene again
to understand the world,
the first speaker will again
point silently out the window
at the hillside in its season,
sunlit, under the snow,
and we will nod silently,
and silently stand and go.

III

As timely as a river
God's timeless life passes
Into this world. It passes
Through bodies, giving life,
And past them, giving death.
The secret fish leaps up
Into the light and is
Again darkened. The sun
Comes from the dark, it lights
The always passing river,
Shines on the great-branched tree,
And goes. Longing and dark,
We are completely filled
With breath of love, in us
Forever incomplete.

IV

The house is cold at dawn.
I wake and build the fires.
The ground is white with snow.

Snow whitens every tree.
No wind has touched the woods.
The deer stand still and look.

V

I know for a while again
the health of self-forgetfulness,
looking out at the sky through
a notch in the valley side,
the black woods wintry on
the hills, small clouds at sunset
passing across. And I know
that this is one of the thresholds
between Earth and Heaven,
from which even I may step
forth from my self and be free.

VI

(Burley Coulter, once in time)
Alone, afoot, in moonless night
Out on the world's edge with his hounds,
What was he looking to set right?
The world sings at its farthest bounds.
To know it does sets right the dark,
And so an old man found his work.

VII

Some had derided him
As unadventurous,
For he would not give up

What he had vowed to keep.
But what he vowed to keep
Even his keeping changed

And, changing, led him far
Beyond what they or he
Foresaw, and made him strange.

What he had vowed to keep
He lost, of course, and yet
Kept in his heart. The things

He vowed to keep, the things
He had in keeping changed,
The things lost in his keeping

That he kept in his heart,
These were his pilgrimage,
Were his adventure, near

And far, at home and in
The world beyond this world.

VIII

We hear way off approaching sounds
Of rain on leaves and on the river:
O blessed rain, bring up the grass
To the tongues of the hungry cattle.

IX

I've come down from the sky
Like some damned ghost, delayed
Too long in time enforced
By fire and by machines,
Returned at last to this
Sweet wooded slope well known
Before, where time flows on
Uncumbered as the wind.

*

No man intended this.
What came here as a gift
We use for good or ill,
For life or waste of life,
But it is as it is.
To the abandoned fields
The trees returned and grew.
They stand and grow. Time comes
To them, time goes, the trees
Stand; the only place
They go is where they are.
These wholly patient ones
Who only stand and wait
For time to come to them,
Who do not go to time,
Stand in eternity.
They stand where they belong.
They do no wrong, and they
Are beautiful. What more

Could we have thought to ask?
Here God and man have rest.

*

I've gone too far toward time,
And now have come back home.
I stand and wait for light,
Flight-weary, growing old,
And grieved for loss of time,
For loss of time's gifts gone
With time forever, taught
By time a timeless love.

*

I stand and wait for light
To open the dark night.
I stand and wait for prayer
To come and find me here.

X

1.

We follow the dead to their graves,
and our long love follows on
beyond, crying to them, not
"Come back!" but merely "Wait!"
In waking thoughts, in dreams
we follow after, calling, "Wait!
Listen! I am older now. I know
now how it was with you
when you were old and I
was only young. I am ready
now to accompany you
in your lonely fear." And they
go on, one by one, as one
by one we go as they have gone.

2.

And yet we all are gathered
in this leftover love,
this longing become the measure
of a joy all mourners know.
An old man's mind is a graveyard
where the dead arise.

Sabbaths 2001

I

He wakes in darkness. All around
are sounds of shifting stones, doors
opening. As if someone had lifted
away a great weight, light
falls on him. He has been asleep or merely
gone. He has known a long suffering
of himself, himself shaped by pain,
his wound of separation he now
no longer minds, for the pain is only himself
now, grown small, become a little growing
longing joy. Joy teaches him
to rise, to stand and move out through
the opening the light has made.
He stands on the green hilltop amid
the cedars, the skewed stones, the earth all
opened doors. Half blind with light, he traces
with his forefinger the moss-grown
furrows of his name, hearing among the others
one woman's cry. She is crying and laughing,
her voice a stream of silver he seems to see:
"Oh, William, honey, is it you? Oh!"

II

Surely it will be for this: the redbud
pink, the wild plum white, yellow
trout lilies in the morning light,
the trees, the pastures turning green.
On the river, quiet at daybreak,
the reflections of the trees, as in
another world, lie across
from shore to shore. Yes, here
is where they will come, the dead,
when they rise from the grave.

III

Ask the world to reveal its quietude —
not the silence of machines when they are still,
but the true quiet by which birdsongs,
trees, bellworts, snails, clouds, storms
become what they are, and are nothing else.

IV

A mind that has confronted ruin for years
Is half or more a ruined mind. Nightmares
Inhabit it, and daily evidence
Of the clean country smeared for want of sense,
Of freedom slack and dull among the free,
Of faith subsumed in idiot luxury,
And beauty beggared in the marketplace
And clear-eyed wisdom bleary with dispraise.

V

The wind of the fall is here.
It is everywhere. It moves
every leaf of every
tree. It is the only motion
of the river. Green leaves
grow weary of their color.
Now evening too is in the air.
The bright hawks of the day
subside. The owls waken.
Small creatures die because
larger creatures are hungry.
How superior to this
human confusion of greed
and creed, blood and fire.

VI

The question before me, now that I
am old, is not how to be dead,
which I know from enough practice,
but how to be alive, as these worn
hills still tell, and some paintings
of Paul Cézanne, and this mere
singing wren, who thinks he's alive
forever, this instant, and may be.

Sabbaths 2002

I

Late winter cold
over the old ground,
mud freezing under
wind and snow,
and above, on the bluffs
the bare woods rattling
in worse wind. Weary,
an old man feeds hay
to the stock at the end
of a winter's day
in a time reduced
to work, hunger, worry,
grief, and as always
war, the killed peace
of the original world.

II

After a mild winter
the new lambs come
in a March as wet, cold,
and unforgiving as any
I remember. Night freezes
continue into April.
But the brave birds risk
a note of hope, and the bold
little wood anemones
lift their pretty blooms
into the cold above
the dead leaves. The sun
grows slowly stronger.
This Sabbath morning, I climb
again to the high woods
and sit down. Toward noon
the wind loses its edge.
Comfort comes.
I eat, and then sleep
in warmth on dry leaves
in a sheltered pocket
of the slope, the wind yet
loud beyond. I sleep
sound among young trees,
among cairns of rocks
piled up by those who cut
older trees to plant

the slope in rows. I wake
thinking of the ones who once
were here, some I knew,
others I know by stories
told and retold. I know
the hard daylong work
that once was done here:
the heat, the long enduring,
the resting and the talk
around the water jug
in shade at the row's end.
Now they are gone, and I
stay on a little while,
the trees, I hope, for longer
this time than before.
I rise from the ground now
more slowly than I used to,
thinking of those I remember
who no longer rise at all
and of those farther back
I never knew even
by story, whose names are lost,
who came by ship from places
whose names are lost.
In distance, like the trees,
the human generations
gather into a wall
nobody sees beyond.
Here where fields were

the woods are, and I come
again into the one time,
the Sabbath time, the timeless
that we pass through
and the woods grows up behind us.

III

We come at last to the dark
and enter in. We are given bodies
newly made out of their absence
from one another in the light
of the ordinary day. We come
to the space between ourselves,
the narrow doorway, and pass through
into the land of the wholly loved.

IV

The Acadian flycatcher, not
a spectacular bird, not a great
singer, is seen only when
alertly watched for. His call
is hardly a song—
a two-syllable squeak you hear
only when you listen for it.
His back is the color of a leaf
in shadow, his belly that
of a leaf in light. He is here
when the leaves are here, belonging
as the leaves belong, is gone when
they go. His is the voice
of this deep place among
the tiers of summer foliage
where three streams come together.
You sit and listen to the voice
of the water, and then you hear
the voice of the bird. He is saying
to his mate, to himself, to whoever
may want to know: "I'm here!"

V

The cherries turn ripe, ripe,
and the birds come: red-headed
and red-bellied woodpeckers,
blue jays, cedar waxwings,
robins—beautiful, hungry, wild
in our domestic tree. I pick
with the birds, gathering the red
cherries alight among the dark
leaves, my hands so sticky
with juice the fruit will hardly
drop from them into the pail.
The birds pick as I pick, all
of us delighted in the weighty heights
—the fruit red ripe, the green leaves,
the blue sky and white clouds,
all tending to flight—making
the most of this sweetness against
the time when there will be none.

VI

In memory: Denise Levertov

Is this the river of life
or death? Both? Both. The force
that brought us here remains
to carry us away.

Wearing its way down,
the river has left us here
on this all-slanting place:
trees, people, animals.
We stand and move a while
in air. A silent, perfect,
inaccessible world
shines sometimes at our feet.

We fall, and are carried away.
Shadowy, shadowy,
we lovers in our vale.

In its darkness the river
has worn the country
into the form it is.
The land is the water's memory.
It remembers in the light
what was made in the dark.

To know what flesh inherits,
learn the art of the little boat,
leave the solid footing,
row out upon the water.

Daylight rests brightly
on the surface of the river.
Sometimes, the air still,
world and sky rest
perfectly upon the water,
quiet as a happy dream.

Sometimes we look through it
shallowly at small fish
quick among the rocks.

In flood opaque, it is
the land's shaker, giver
and taker, maker of this place.

Sometimes when the wind
stirs, the surface is all
an impenetrable glitter, without
image or depth. Beneath
that clutter of light, our floating
eyesight, the river is dark.

Lives are lived down there
in the airless shadow where
to live long, for us, would be
to die. Excluded, we watch
the surface which divides.

From time to time we see
a long fish leap like an angel up
into common day. The dark
life shines in the air
in a cloud of bright spray.

The light flows toward the earth,
the river toward the sea,
and these do not change.
The air changes, as the mind
changes at a word from the light,
a flash from the dark.

In the curtain of wild grape
along the steep shore,
a yellow warbler appeared, disappeared
like a bright stitch. I remember
that from forty years ago.

Bedeviled by the engines
of the utterly displaced
who come to enjoy the quiet
by making noise in it,
this is the river of the birth
of my mind and inspiration,
my watching many years
here where I have made my toils.

And now I must imagine it
rising, light drawn, invisibly
up into the air.

At dusk the gray heron flies
home among the trees
and then is hidden
from everything but itself,
at peace with the day
and the coming dark.

VII

The flocking blackbirds fly across
the river, appearing above the trees
on one side, disappearing beyond
the trees on the other side. The flock
undulates in passage beneath the opening
of white sky that seems no wider
than the river. It is mid August.
The year is changing. The summer's young
are grown and strong in flight. Soon now
it will be fall. The frost will come.
To one who has watched here many years,
all of this is familiar. And yet
none of it has ever happened
before as it is happening now.

VIII

Every afternoon the old turtle
crawls up out of the river
along the trunk of a drowned tree
that slants out of the watery dark
into the sun and the wind.
In the wind and the sun he gets dry
and ceases to shine. He grows warm.
He looks slowly this way and that way.
He thinks slowly, and his thought
passes from satiety to hunger.
And so he lets himself sink back
down out of the air and light.

IX

All yesterday afternoon I sat
here by the river while the holiday
boats sped by. Their wake
beat on the shores, muddying
the water, their sleek hulls
rocking and pounding in the wake
of other boats, the engines filling
the air with torment. They will come
again today and again tomorrow,
for this is Labor Day weekend,
a time to celebrate with restlessness
the possibility of rest always
farther on. But this morning I came
again at first light. The river
had cleared. It lay still from bend
to bend. The night birds were passing
homeward ahead of the day. An owl
trilled once, and then a wren woke
and sang. The herons stalked
soundlessly the dusky shallows. Quietly,
quietly, the river received
the forgiveness of the new dawn.

X

Teach me work that honors Thy work,
the true economies of goods and words,
to make my arts compatible
with the songs of the local birds.

Teach me patience beyond work
and, beyond patience, the blest
Sabbath of Thy unresting love
which lights all things and gives rest.

Sabbaths 2003

I

The woods is white with snow.
The shy birds come and go
Between feeder and trees.
Titmice and chickadees
By right of flight survive,
I by the heavy stove.

II

The kindly faithful light returns.
Morning returns and the forgiving season.
The pastures turn green, again. Blossom
and leafbud gentle the harsh woods.
The warm breezes return to the cold river.
The phoebe returns to the porch.
And I return again to my window
where I have sat at my work all winter.
In the fortieth year of my work in this room
I sit without working and look out,
an old man, into the young light.

III Look Out

Come to the window, look out, and see
the valley turning green in remembrance
of all springs past and to come, the woods
perfecting with immortal patience
the leaves that are the work of all of time,
the sycamore whose white limbs shed
the history of a man's life with their old bark,
the river under the morning's breath quivering
like the touched skin of a horse, and you will see
also the shadow cast upon it by fire, the war
that lights its way by burning the earth.

Come to your windows, people of the world,
look out at whatever you see wherever you are,
and you will see dancing upon it that shadow.
You will see that your place, wherever it is,
your house, your garden, your shop, your forest, your farm,
bears the shadow of its destruction by war
which is the economy of greed which is plunder
which is the economy of wrath which is fire.
The Lords of War sell the earth to buy fire,
they sell the water and air of life to buy fire.
They are little men grown great by willingness
to drive whatever exists into its perfect absence.
Their intention to destroy any place is solidly founded
upon their willingness to destroy every place.

Every household of the world is at their mercy,
the households of the farmer and the otter and the owl

are at their mercy. They have no mercy.
Having hate, they can have no mercy.
Their greed is the hatred of mercy.
Their pockets jingle with the small change of the poor.
Their power is their willingness to destroy
everything for knowledge which is money
which is power which is victory
which is ashes sown by the wind.

Leave your windows and go out, people of the world,
go into the streets, go into the fields, go into the woods
and along the streams. Go together, go alone.
Say no to the Lords of War which is Money
which is Fire. Say no by saying yes
to the air, to the earth, to the trees,
yes to the grasses, to the rivers, to the birds
and the animals and every living thing, yes
to the small houses, yes to the children. Yes.

IV

The little stream sings
in the crease of the hill.
It is the water of life. It knows
nothing of death, nothing.
And this is the morning
of Christ's resurrection.
The tomb is empty. There is
no death. Death is our illusion,
our wish to belong only
to ourselves, which is our freedom
to kill one another.
From this sleep may we too
rise, as out of the dark grave.

V

The politics of illusion, of death's money,
possesses us. This is the Hell, this
the nightmare into which Christ descended
from the cross, from which also he woke
and rose, striding godly forth, so free
that He appeared to Mary Magdalene
to be only the gardener walking about
in the new day, among the flowers.

VI
(for Jonathan Williams)

The yellow-throated warbler, the highest remotest voice
of this place, sings in the tops of the tallest sycamores,
but one day he came twice to the railing of my porch
where I sat at work above the river. He was too close
to see with binoculars. Only the naked eye could take him in,
a bird more beautiful than every picture of himself,
more beautiful than himself killed and preserved
by the most skilled taxidermist, more beautiful
than any human mind, so small and inexact,
could hope ever to remember. My mind became
beautiful by the sight of him. He had the beauty only
of himself alive in the only moment of his life.
He had upon him like a light the whole
beauty of the living world that never dies.

VII

This, then, is to be the way? Freedom's candle will be
snuffed out by freedom's sworn defenders, chanting
hourly the praise of freedom. Their praise
will console the free waking in their prisons
when the Bill of Rights has at last
dissolved in the indifference of the great Self
of force. When the strong have perfected their triumph
over the weak, great symphonies will still
be played in the concert halls and on the radio
to console the forgetful and the undisturbed; the doors
will still stand open at the art museums,
rewarding the oppressed for their oppression; poets
will still intone fluently their songs
of themselves, to reward the fearful for their fear. Oh,
the lofty artists of sound, of shape and color,
of words, will still accept proudly their jobs
in universities, their prizes, grants, and awards.
On the day that ugliness is perfected in rubble
and blood, beauty and the love of beauty will
still be praised by those well paid to praise it.

*

When they cannot speak freely in defiance
of wealth self-elected to righteousness,
let the arts of pleasure and beauty cease.
Let every poet and singer of joy be dumb.
When those in power by owning all the words
have made them mean nothing, let silence
speak for us. When freedom's light goes out, let color

drain from all paintings into gray puddles
on the museum floor. When every ear awaits only
the knock on the door in the dark midnight,
let all the orchestras sound just one long note of woe.

VIII

All that patriotism requires, and all that it can be,
is eagerness to maintain intact and incorrupt
the founding principles of the nation, and to preserve
undiminished the land and the people. If national conduct
forsakes these aims, it is one's patriotic duty
to say so and to oppose. What else have we to live for?

IX

After the campaign of the killing machines
the place, which could be any place,
was heaped with corpses, dismembered and stinking.
For them the great simplification had come
and the fear of suffering, at least, at last was finished.
But the one we have remembered longest was the one
who survived, who was pulled free,
bloody with his own blood and the blood
of the reeking dead who, dying, had sheltered him
— the one who to his horror found that the little light
of our world is beautiful and holy,
and he must live.

X

But do the Lords of War in fact
hate the world? That would be easy
to bear, if so. If they hated
their children and the flowers
that grow in the warming light,
that would be easy to bear. For then
we could hate the haters
and be right. What is hard
is to imagine the Lords of War
may love the things that they destroy.

XI

It is late November, Thanksgiving,
and the slow rain falls as all day
it has fallen. The mists drift
in the treetops along Camp Branch.
The ewe flock grazes the green slope
as in a dream of a painting
by Samuel Palmer. There is no wind.
It is completely quiet. From the distance
comes only the sound of the branch
flowing in its wooded hollow, old,
old, and new, unidentifying the day
and the man giving his thanks.

Sabbaths 2004

I

(After the painting Jacob's Dream *by William Blake and Genesis 28: 11–17)*

A young man leaving home
For long years to be gone
Might fall asleep and dream,
His head upon a stone.

A stair appears that bends
In spiral toward the light,
The bright Orb where it ends,
Though he sleeps through the night,

Darkened, below the stars.
Angels in constant motion
Walk up and down the stairs.
Delight and clear devotion

Make graceful all they do.
The light and dark are bound,
Heaven to all below,
Bright stair and stony ground

In one light joined. In sleep
The dreamer wakes. He sees
Above the stars the deep
Of Heaven opened. Is

He living, then, his part
Of Heaven's earthly life?
And what shall be the art
By which this sight can live?

Darkened upon the earth,
He fills with light, is made
A witness to high Truth
And so a man afraid.

His land—this meager sod,
These stones, this low estate—
Is the household of God.
And it is Heaven's gate.

II

They come singly, the little streams,
Out of their solitude. They bear
In their rough fall a spate of gleams
That glance and dance in morning air.

They come singly, and coming go
Ever downward toward the river
Into whose dark abiding flow
They come, now quieted, together.

In dark they mingle and are made
At one with light in highest flood
Embodied and inhabited,
The budded branch as red as blood.

III

They are fighting again the war to end war,
And the ewe flock, bred in October, brings forth
in March. This so far remains, this pain
and renewal, whatever war is being fought.
We go through the annual passage of birth
and death, triumph and heartbreak, love
and exasperation, mud, milk, mucus, and blood.
Yet once more the young ewe stands with her lambs
in the dawnlight, the lambs well-suckled
and dry. There is no happiness like this.

The window again welcomes in the light
of lengthening days. The river in its old groove
passes again beneath opening leaves.
In their brevity, between cold and shade,
flowers again brighten the woods floor.

This then may be the prayer without ceasing,
this beauty and gratitude, this moment.

IV

(Jayber Crow in old age)
To think of gathering all
the sorrows of Port William
into myself, and so
sparing the others:
What freedom! What joy!

V

I built a timely room beside the river,
The slope beneath descending to the water.
Some mornings it is vibrant with the glance
Of sunlight brightened on the little waves
The wind drives shoreward, stirring leaves and branches
Over the roof also. It is a room
Of pictures and of memories of some
Who are no more in time, and of the absent
And of the present the unresting thoughts.
It is a room as timely as the body,
As frail, to shelter love's eternal work,
Always unfinished, here at water's edge,
The work of beauty, faith, and gratitude
Eternally alive in time. Around
The walls the trees like waves, like men,
Come up, come up, expend themselves, and die.
The water shines back the unending sky.

VI

Up in the blown-down woods
you try to imagine the tornado
cracking through the trees
while you slept, branches
and birds' eggs whirling
in the dark. You can't do it.
You can imagine the place
as it was, and as it is.
The moment of transformation,
the presence of creation,
itself is beyond your reach.

VII

Dee Rice Amyx, 1910–2004

A gracious lady came to us
and favored us by receiving
kindly our care of her
at the end of all her days.

She was a lady made graceful
beyond what we had known
by the welcome she gave to death,
her guest, whom she made unfearful

by her fearlessness, having no further
use for herself as we had known her.

VIII

It takes all time to show eternity,
The longest shine of every perishing spark,
And every word and cry of every tongue
Must form the Word that calls the darkest dark

Of this world to its lasting dawn. Toward
That rising hour we bear our single hearts
Estranged as islands parted in the sea,
Our broken knowledge and our scattered arts.

As separate as fireflies or night windows,
We piece a foredream of the gathered light
Infinitely small and great to shelter all,
Silenced into song, blinded into sight.

IX

I mistook your white head for a flower
down there among the tall grasses
and flowers of the garden border.
And then I knew you, your years
upon you like a crown of glory.

X

An old man, who has been on many days
a man of the woods, has come again
to this place where three streams join, where
once he sat in his pleasure under the tall trees
and the world's light shone from every leaf,

where now a great wind has blown, and he
is alone still upright, his old companions
all broken and brought down. It is the place
of endings he has come to, of the world's end
that is always near, always here. "Farewell,"

he says. "Welcome," he says. For it is the place
also of the world's beginning, ever here, for here
there is again a living darkness underfoot,
a small wind is moving farther into time, and here
he is, astir among the fallen.

INDEX OF TITLES AND FIRST LINES
(Titles are in italics, first lines in roman.)

ACKNOWLEDGMENTS

"To Tanya on My Sixtieth Birthday," "Sabbaths 1998," "The woods is white with snow," "The kindly faithful light returns," "The little stream sings," "The politics of illusion," "When they cannot speak freely in defiance" from "This, then, is to be the way? Freedom's candle will be," and "It is late November, Thanksgiving" of "Sabbaths 2003" first appeared in *The Sewanee Review*.

"To a Writer of Reputation," "Burley Coulter's Song for Kate Helen Branch," "In Art Rowenberry's Barn," and "The Rejected Husband" first appeared in *Chronicles*.

"Dust," "June Wind," "How to Be a Poet," "Why," and "They" first appeared in *Poetry*.

"The Future" first appeared in *Limestone*.

"The Millennium" was first published by the Kentucky Folk Art Center.

"Sonata at Payne Hollow," "Cathedral," "Dante," "The Leader," and "A Position" first appeared in *The Southern Review*.

"The Fact" and "All" first appeared in *Ploughshares*.

"Original Sin" first appeared in *Wind*.

"Words" first appeared in *The Progressive*.

"Some Further Words" first appeared in *The American Poetry Review*.

"A Small Theology" first appeared in *The Cresset*.

"In a Country Once Forested" first appeared in *Mars Hill Review*.

"Sabbaths 1999" and "Sabbaths 2000" first appeared in *The Hudson Review*.

"I know for a while again" of "Sabbaths 2000" also appeared in *Wilderness*.

"Sabbaths 2002" was published as a chapbook by Larkspur Press in Monterey, Kentucky.

"Look Out" and "An old man, who has been on many days" first appeared in *Temenos Academy Review 8*.

Wendell Berry is grateful to the editors of all these publications, as he is also to all the staff of Shoemaker and Hoard for the present volume.